THE MYERS-BRIGGS TYPE INDICATOR WAS DEVELOPED BY:

KATHARINE C. BRIGGS

and

ISABEL BRIGGS MYERS

D0001301

IT IS BASED ON...

C.G. JUNG'S "PSYCHOLOGICAL TYPES"

THE MYERS-BRIGGS TYPE INDICATOR REPORTS SOME OF YOUR KEY

PREFERENCES, TENDENCIES, CHARACTERISTICS

BUT NOT

ALL

OF THEM

YOU DECIDE

HOW **ACCURATE**
THE REPORT IS

FOR **YOU**

THE
FOUR
PREFERENCE
SCALES

ARE....

EXTRAVERSION OR INTROVERSION

SENSING OR INTUITION

THINKING OR FEELING

JUDGMENT OR PERCEPTION

EXTRAVERSION AND INTROVERSION
ARE COMPLEMENTARY ATTITUDES
TOWARD THE WORLD

E

An Extravert's Essential Stimulation Is From The
Environment—The Outer World Of People And Things.

I

An Introvert's Essential Stimulation Is From
Within—The Inner World Of Thoughts And Reflections.

• •

Both Attitudes Are Used By Everyone, But One Is
Usually Preferred And Better Developed

EXTRAVERSION
Tendencies & Characteristics

Feels Pulled Outward
By External Claims
And Conditions

Energized By
Other People,
External Experiences

INTROVERSION
Tendencies & Characteristics

Feels Pushed Inward
By External Claims
And Intrusions

Energized By
Inner Resources,
Internal Experiences

EXTRAVERSION

Tendencies &
Characteristics

Acts, Then
(Maybe) Reflects

Is Often Friendly,
Talkative, Easy To Know

INTROVERSION

Tendencies &
Characteristics

Reflects, Then
(Maybe) Acts

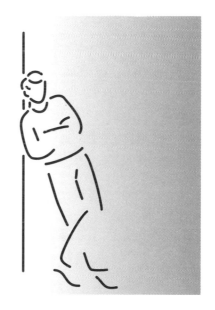

Is Often Reserved,
Quiet, Hard to Know

EXTRAVERSION
Tendencies &
Characteristics

INTROVERSION
Tendencies &
Characteristics

Expresses Thoughts And Emotions Freely (May Be At Risk Of Saying Too Much)

Keeps Thoughts And Emotions Private (May Be At Risk Of Saying Too Little)

Needs Relationships

Needs Privacy

EXTRAVERSION
Tendencies & Characteristics

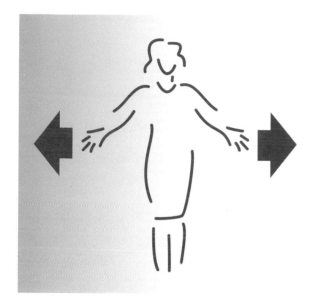

Gives Breadth
To Life

Es May Seem
Shallow To **I**s

INTROVERSION
Tendencies & Characteristics

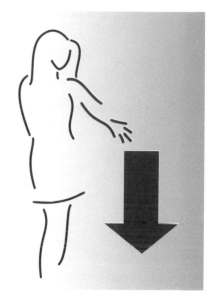

Gives Depth
To Life

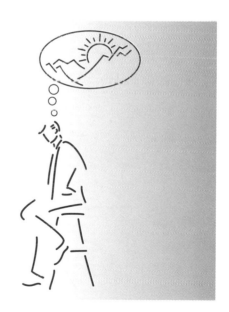

Is May Seem
Withdrawn To **E**s

EXTRAVERSION

INTROVERSION

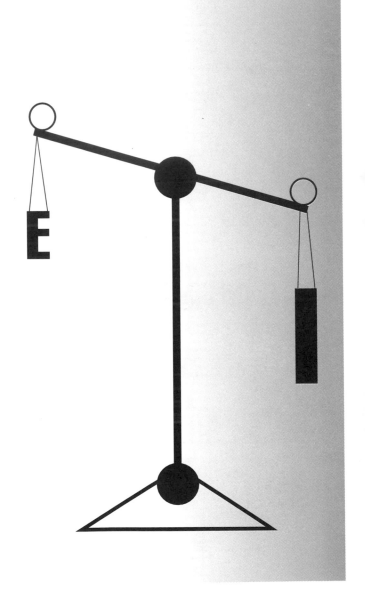

Needs Introversion
For Balance

Needs Extraversion
For Balance

SOME KEY WORDS

E

EXTRAVERSION

ACTIVE

OUTWARD

SOCIABLE

PEOPLE

MANY

EXPRESSIVE

BREADTH

I

INTROVERSION

REFLECTIVE

INWARD

RESERVED

PRIVACY

FEW

QUIET

DEPTH

These Characteristics Often Develop From **E** And **I** Preferences. Some Of Them May Be True Of You.

EXTRAVERTS USE BOTH E AND I, BUT PREFER E

INTROVERTS USE BOTH E AND I, BUT PREFER I

HOW CLEAR IS **YOUR** PREFERENCE

E ————————————————— **I**

Clear - Moderate - Slight | Slight - Moderate - Clear

SENSING AND INTUITION
ARE WAYS OF
TAKING IN INFORMATION

S

The Sensing Function Takes In Information By Way of the Five
Senses - Sight, Sound, Touch, Taste, And Smell.

N

The Intuiting Function Processes Information By Way
Of A "Sixth Sense" Or Insight.

• •

Both Ways Of Perceiving And Taking In Information Are Used By
Everyone, But One Is Usually Preferred And Better Developed.

SENSING
Tendencies & Characteristics

INTUITION
Tendencies & Characteristics

Sees Specific Parts And Pieces

Sees Patterns And Relationships

Lives In The Present, Enjoying What's There

Lives Toward The Future, Anticipating What Might Be

SENSING
Tendencies & Characteristics

**Prefers Handling
Practical Matters**

**Likes Things That Are
Definite, Measurable**

INTUITION
Tendencies & Characteristics

**Prefers Imagining
Possibilities**

**Likes Opportunities
For Being Inventive**

SENSING
Tendencies & Characteristics

Starts At The Beginning,
Takes A Step At A Time

Works Hands-On With
The Parts To Understand
The Overall Design

INTUITION
Tendencies & Characteristics

Jumps In Anywhere,
Leaps Over Steps

Studies The Overall Design
To Understand How The
Parts Fit Together

SENSING
Tendencies & Characteristics

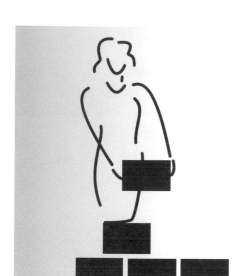

Enjoys Using And Refining
The Known And Familiar

Ss May Seem Materialistic
and Literal-Minded To **N**s

INTUITION
Tendencies & Characteristics

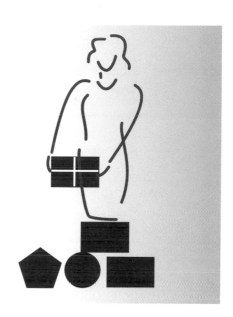

Enjoys Experimenting With
The New And Different

Ns May Seem Fickle,
Impractical Dreamers To **S**s

SENSING   INTUITION

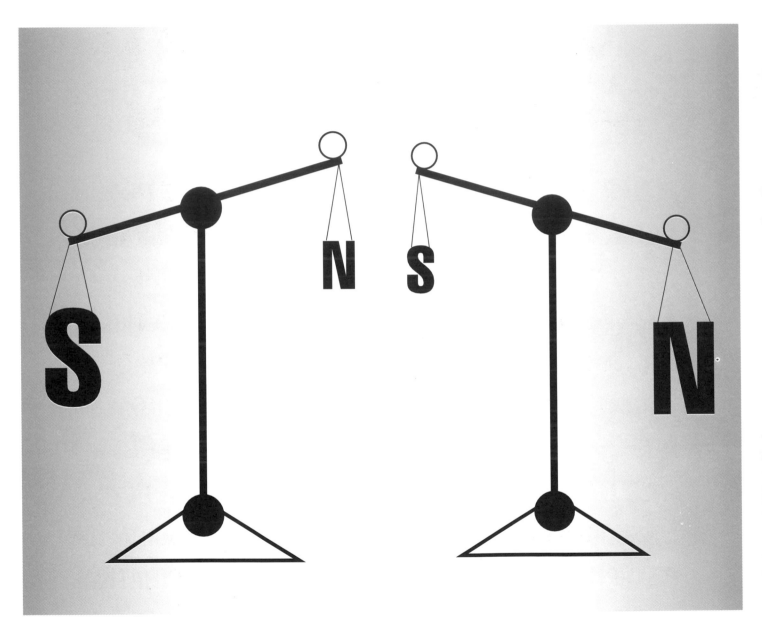

Needs Intuition
For Balance

Needs Sensing
For Balance

SOME KEY WORDS

S

SENSING
DETAILS
PRESENT
PRACTICAL
FACTS
SEQUENTIAL
DIRECTIONS
REPETITION
ENJOYMENT
PERSPIRATION
CONSERVE
LITERAL

N

INTUITION
PATTERNS
FUTURE
IMAGINATIVE
INNOVATIONS
RANDOM
HUNCHES
VARIETY
ANTICIPATION
INSPIRATION
CHANGE
FIGURATIVE

These Characteristics Often Develop From **S** And **N** Preferences.
Some Of Them May Be True Of You.

SENSING TYPES USE BOTH S AND N, BUT PREFER S

INTUITIVE TYPES USE BOTH S AND N, BUT PREFER N

HOW CLEAR IS YOUR PREFERENCE

S   **N**

Clear - Moderate - Slight | Slight - Moderate - Clear

THINKING AND FEELING
ARE WAYS OF
MAKING DECISIONS

T

Thinking Is The Mental Process That Decides
On The Basis Of Logical Analysis.

F

Feeling Is The Mental Process That Decides
On The Basis Of Evaluating Relative Worth.

• •

Both Ways Of Deciding And Evaluating Are Used By Everyone,
But One Is Usually Preferred And Better Developed.

THINKING
Tendencies & Characteristics

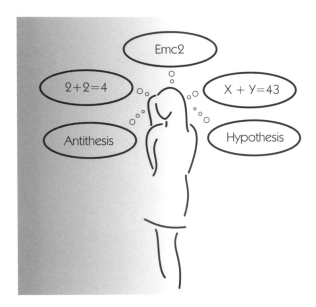

Decides With The Head

Goes By Logic

FEELING
Tendencies & Characteristics

Decides With The Heart

Goes By Personal Convictions

THINKING
Tendencies & Characteristics

Concerned With
Principles Such As
Truth, Justice

Sees Things As An
On-Looker From Outside
A Situation

FEELING
Tendencies & Characteristics

Concerned With
Values Such As
Relationships, Harmony

Sees Things As A
Participant From Within
A Situation

THINKING
Tendencies & Characteristics

FEELING
Tendencies & Characteristics

Takes A Long
Range View

Takes An Immediate
And Personal View

Spontaneously
Critiques

Spontaneously
Appreciates

THINKING
Tendencies & Characteristics

Good At
Analyzing Plans

Ts May Seem Cold And
Condescending To **F**s

FEELING
Tendencies & Characteristics

Good At
Understanding People

Fs May Seem
Fuzzy-Minded and
Emotional To **T**s

THINKING

FEELING

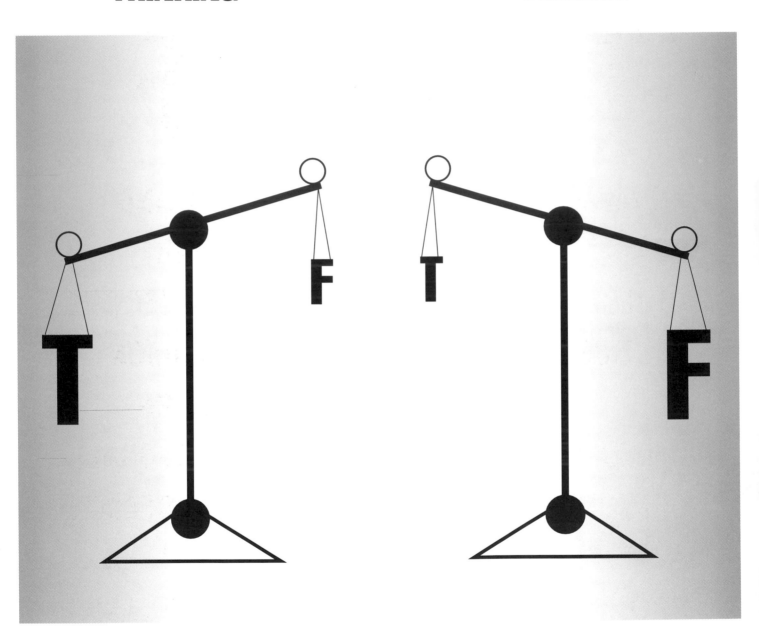

Needs Feeling
For Balance

Needs Thinking
For Balance

SOME KEY WORDS

T

THINKING

HEAD

OBJECTIVE

JUSTICE

COOL

IMPERSONAL

CRITIQUE

ANALYZE

PRECISE

PRINCIPLES

F

FEELING

HEART

SUBJECTIVE

HARMONY

CARING

PERSONAL

APPRECIATE

EMPATHIZE

PERSUASIVE

VALUES

These Characteristics Often Develop From **T** And **F** Preferences.
Some Of Them May Be True Of You.

THINKING TYPES USE BOTH T AND F, BUT PREFER T

FEELING TYPES USE BOTH T AND F, BUT PREFER F

HOW CLEAR IS

YOUR

PREFERENCE

? ? ? ?

T   **F**

Clear - Moderate - Slight | Slight - Moderate - Clear

JUDGMENT AND PERCEPTION

ARE COMPLEMENTARY LIFESTYLES

J

A Judging Lifestyle Is Decisive, Planned, And Orderly.

P

A Perceiving Lifestyle Is Flexible, Adaptable, And Spontaneous.

• •

Both Attitudes Are Part Of Everyone's Lifestyle,
But One Is Usually Preferred And Better Developed.

JUDGMENT
Tendencies & Characteristics

PERCEPTION
Tendencies & Characteristics

Prefers An
Organized Lifestyle

Prefers A
Flexible Lifestyle

Likes Definite
Order And Structure

Likes Going
With The Flow

JUDGMENT
Tendencies & Characteristics

PERCEPTION
Tendencies & Characteristics

Likes To Have Life
Under Control

Prefers To Experience
Life As It Happens

Enjoys Being Decisive

Enjoys Being Curious,
Discovering Surprises

JUDGMENT
Tendencies & Characteristics

PERCEPTION
Tendencies & Characteristics

Likes Clear Limits And Categories

Likes Freedom To Explore Without Limits

Feels Comfortable Establishing Closure

Feels Comfortable Maintaining Openness

JUDGMENT
Tendencies & Characteristics

Handles Deadlines,
Plans In Advance

Js May Seem
Demanding, Rigid,
Uptight To **P**s

PERCEPTION
Tendencies & Characteristics

Meets Deadlines By
Last Minute Rush

Ps May Seem
Disorganized, Messy,
Irresponsible To **J**s

JUDGMENT

PERCEPTION

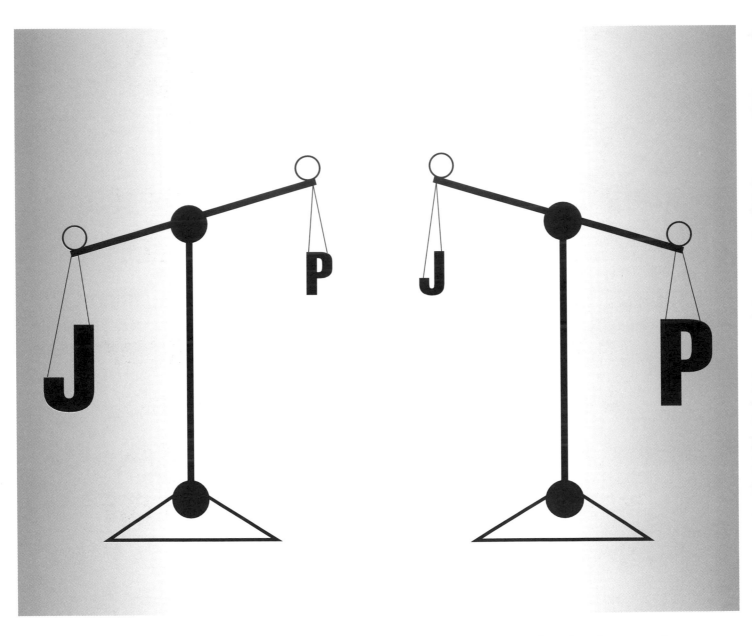

Needs Perception
For Balance

Needs Judgment
For Balance

SOME KEY WORDS

J

JUDGMENT

ORGANIZED

STRUCTURE

CONTROL

DECISIVE

DELIBERATE

CLOSURE

PLAN

DEADLINES

PRODUCTIVE

P

PERCEPTION

FLEXIBLE

FLOW

EXPERIENCE

CURIOUS

SPONTANEOUS

OPENNESS

WAIT

DISCOVERIES

RECEPTIVE

These Characteristics Often Develop From **J** And **P** Preferences.
Some Of Them May Be True Of You.

JUDGING TYPES USE BOTH J AND P, BUT PREFER J

PERCEIVING TYPES USE BOTH J AND P, BUT PREFER P

HOW CLEAR IS YOUR PREFERENCE

J   P

Clear - Moderate - Slight | Slight - Moderate - Clear

WHEN COMBINED,
YOUR FOUR PREFERENCES

EXTRAVERSION OR INTROVERSION

SENSING OR INTUITION

THINKING OR FEELING

JUDGMENT OR PERCEPTION

INDICATE YOUR

PREFERENCE TYPE

THE **MBTI** DOES NOT ASSESS...

APTITUDE

"NORMALCY"

PSYCHOLOGICAL
ILLNESS

MATURITY

EMOTIONS

PHYSICAL
ILLNESS

TRAUMA

SKILL

STRESS

INTELLIGENCE

LEARNING

"TYPE"

IS HELPFUL IN UNDERSTANDING YOURSELF AND OTHER PEOPLE

BUT REMEMBER...

EVERYONE IS AN INDIVIDUAL

CONTRIBUTION MADE BY EACH PREFERENCE TO EACH TYPE

ISTJ
I Depth Of Concentration

S Reliance On Facts

T Logic And Analysis

J Organization

ISFJ
I Depth Of Concentration

S Reliance On Facts

F Warmth And Sympathy

J Organization

INFJ
I Depth Of Concentration

N Grasp Of Possibilities

F Warmth And Sympathy

J Organization

INTJ
I Depth Of Concentration

N Grasp Of Possibilities

T Logic And Analysis

J Organization

ISTP
I Depth Of Concentration

S Reliance On Facts

T Logic And Analysis

P Adaptability

ISFP
I Depth Of Concentration

S Reliance On Facts

F Warmth And Sympathy

P Adaptability

INFP
I Depth Of Concentration

N Grasp Of Possibilities

F Warmth And Sympathy

P Adaptability

INTP
I Depth Of Concentration

N Grasp Of Possibilities

T Logic And Analysis

P Adaptability

ESTP
E Breadth Of Interests

S Reliance On Facts

T Logic And Analysis

P Adaptability

ESFP
E Breadth Of Interests

S Reliance On Facts

F Warmth And Sympathy

P Adaptability

ENFP
E Breadth Of Interests

N Grasp Of Possibilities

F Warmth And Sympathy

P Adaptability

ENTP
E Breadth Of Interests

N Grasp Of Possibilities

T Logic And Analysis

P Adaptability

ESTJ
E Breadth Of Interests

S Reliance On Facts

T Logic And Analysis

J Organization

ESFJ
E Breadth Of Interests

S Reliance On Facts

F Warmth And Sympathy

J Organization

ENFJ
E Breadth Of Interests

N Grasp Of Possibilities

F Warmth And Sympathy

J Organization

ENTJ
E Breadth Of Interests

N Grasp Of Possibilities

T Logic And Analysis

J Organization

EACH OF THESE SIXTEEN TYPES IS GIFTED AND VALUABLE